THE Great Basin for KIDS

by Gretchen M. Baker

Illustrated by Matthew Schenk

for Matthew and Emma

Thanks to Craig Baker, Andrea Daney, Jenny Hamilton, Roberta Moore, Robert and Germaine Schenk, and Clare Sorenson for their helpful comments and encouragement.

ISBN 9-781499-688023

Photo credits: cover, pronghorns, Jenny Hamilton; p. 5 Mt. Whitney, Geographer, Wikipedia; background Features of the Great Basin, Jenny Hamilton; p. 8 Lehman Cave, Peter Schenk; p. 10 volcano, USGS; background, People of the Great Basin, Brandi Roberts; background, Above the Great Basin, Brandi Roberts. All other photos by the author.

Map credit: Tom Patterson

Table of Contents

What is the Great Basin?.. 4

Features of the Great Basin

Fossils... 6
Caves... 8
Volcanic Features 10
Glaciers 12
Huge Lakes 14
Sand Dunes 16

Habitats of the Great Basin

Sagebrush..18
Playas 20
Mountain Forests 22
The High Country 24
Wet Places 26

People of the Great Basin

Native Americans 28
Explorers and Settlers... 30
The Pony Express 32
Miners 34
Cowboys 36

Above the Great Basin

Night Skies.. 38

Test Yourself... 40

What is the Great Basin?

The Great Basin is an area where no water drains to the oceans. The Great Basin covers almost 200,000 square miles, including parts of Nevada, Utah, California, Oregon, Idaho, and Wyoming.

The biggest cities are Salt Lake City, Utah; Reno, Nevada; and Victorville, California. The Great Basin is not just one basin. Hundreds of basins are separated by mountain ranges.

The term *Great Basin Desert* is used to describe a portion of the Great Basin area based on plants and animals that live there. The most common plant in the Great Basin Desert is the sagebrush shrub.

Most of the Great Basin Desert receives about ten inches of rain or snow each year. Some places within the Great Basin Desert are even drier and are also called a desert, such as the Black Rock Desert and the Great Salt Lake Desert.

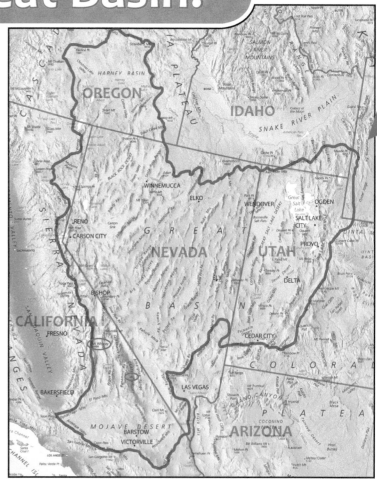

MAP LEGEND

——— *Boundary line of The Great Basin*

——— *State border lines*

The Great Basin contains the highest and lowest points in the lower 48 United States: Mount Whitney (14,494 feet/4420 m) and Badwater Basin (-282 feet/-86 m). That's a difference in elevation of almost 3 miles (5 km)! Find them on the map!

Activity: Great Basin Drainage

Get a big cookie sheet with rims—this signifies the entire Great Basin. Use play dough or clay to make lines of mountains on the cookie sheet, with space in between each line. Then make it rain (sprinkle water) over the mountains. Watch how the water flows down the mountains to the basins, but does not overflow the cookie sheet. This represents how water stays in the Great Basin. It doesn't flow out of the boundaries to the ocean.

Fossils

Much of the rock found in the Great Basin mountains formed hundreds of millions of years ago when a shallow sea covered the area. Various creatures lived and died in the sea, and some became fossils. The Great Basin has a wide variety of fossils, and the many cliffs and rock out-croppings have made it an easy place to find them. Looking for fossils is a good way to learn geology, because fossils are only found in certain rock layers.

Ichthyosaur fossil at the Paleontology Museum at Brigham Young University in Provo, Utah.

FUN FACT: Nevada's state fossil is the ichthyosaur, a giant marine reptile that lived during the time of the dinosaurs. The first complete ichthyosaur was found in England by a 12-year old girl. Paleontologists, scientists who study fossils, continue to learn more about ichthyosaurs and other plants and animals that used to live in the Great Basin.

Activity: Make a Fake Fossil

Get some clay or play dough and some small items such as a seashells, pinecones, leaves, animal bones, or feathers. One type of fossil is the imprint of a plant or animal.

1. Take one of your items and push it gently into a circle of clay, then remove it.

2. Put your fossil in a safe place to dry. After a few hours, it will be hard and look like a fossil.

3. For extra fun, bury it in a sandbox for your friends to find.

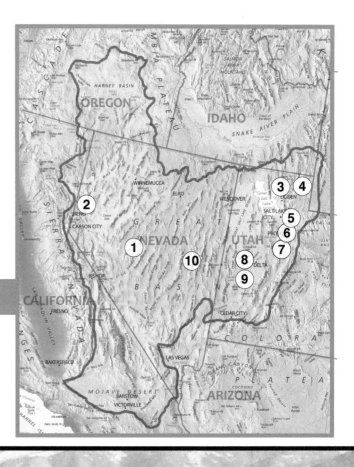

Places To Visit To See Fossils

1 Berlin-Ichthyosaur State Park, near Gabbs, Nevada

2 W.M. Keck Museum, Reno, Nevada

3 George S. Eccles Dinosaur Park, Ogden, Utah

4 Weber State Museum of Natural Science, Ogden, Utah

5 Natural History Museum of Utah, Salt Lake City

6 Museum of Ancient Life, Lehi, Utah

7 Brigham Young University Paleontology Museum, Provo, Utah

8 Great Basin Museum, Delta, Utah

9 U-Dig Fossils near Delta, Utah

10 White Pine Public Museum, Ely, Nevada

Caves

Lehman Cave in Great Basin National Park, Nevada.

You can look inside some of the mountains by going into a cave. A cave is usually formed by water and carbonic acid dissolving away limestone rock. Some passages were dissolved away for sufficient time that they are big enough for people to walk through them. After the rock layer was hollowed out, in some caves water and dissolved limestone created stalactites, stalagmites, flowstone, and other cave formations. Other caves remained dry, with no formations. Some caves are vertical, meaning that you must rappel down a rope to enter them and climb up the rope to reach the surface.

FUN FACT: Cave biologists, scientists who study life in caves, have learned that some cave biota that stay underground their entire lives do not have eyes. They have evolved to live in total darkness. Many are all white, as they need no pigment to protect them from the sun. Some have longer appendages, such as legs or antennae, so they can feel their way around better.

Activity: Make Your Own Cave

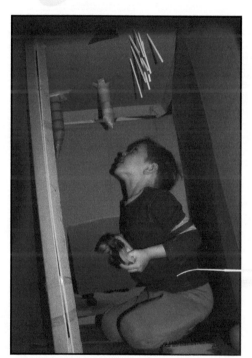

Make cave formations, bats, and cave creatures out of paper and straws and tape them in the box. Put on a headlamp and visit your own cave, making sure that you don't squish any of the animals or damage any of the beautiful formations.

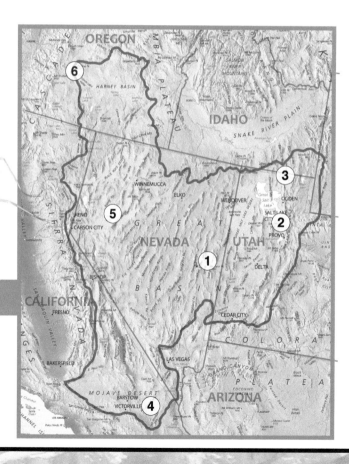

Caves to Visit

(1) Lehman Cave in Great Basin National Park, Baker, Nevada

(2) Timpanogos Cave National Monument, American Fork, Utah

(3) Minnetonka Cave, St. Charles, Idaho

(4) Mitchell Caverns Natural Preserve, Providence Mountains, California

(5) Hidden Cave Archeological Site, Fallon, Nevada

(6) Lava River Cave in Newberry National Volcanic Monument, Bend, Oregon

Volcanic Features

The Great Basin had several periods when volcanoes, cinder cones, and vents spewed material and oozed lava over the land. Some erupted as recently as a few hundred years ago. We can see lava fields, lava tubes, cinder cones, and volcanic rock in many places in the Great Basin. Volcanic rocks, such as rhyolite, tuff, and lava, cover more than twenty percent of the Great Basin.

Lunar Crater, off Highway 6 in central Nevada.

FUN FACT: Where is the next volcanic eruption in the Great Basin going to take place? Some vulcanologists, scientists who study volcanoes, think it could be the Long Valley Caldera, home of Mono and Inyo Craters, north of Bishop, California. One past eruption ejected nearly 500 times the material Mount St. Helens did when it erupted, and ash was blown as far away as Nebraska and Kansas.

Activity: Volcanic Eruption

Ready to make a volcano explode? You can simulate one by burying a water bottle in a pile of dirt. Then add 2 tablespoons baking soda and 2 cups vinegar. Stand back and watch!

Places To Visit To See Volcanic Features

1. Mono Craters, California
2. Newberry National Volcanic Monument, Oregon
3. Diamond Craters, Oregon
4. Lunar Crater, Nevada
5. Black Rock Desert, Utah

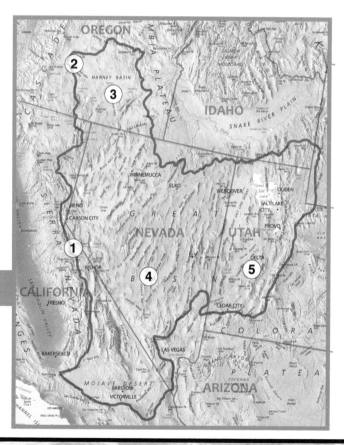

Glaciers

Glaciers form when more snow falls than melts. The heavy snow compacts into ice, which starts flowing downhill. A good description of glaciers is "rivers of ice." At one time (during the Pleistocene, 15,000-35,000 years ago), glaciers were present in about thirty of the mountain ranges in the Great Basin. Today only one ice glacier

Wheeler Cirque Rock Glacier, Great Basin National Park, Nevada.

is left: a tiny one in Great Basin National Park. We can see signs glaciers left behind in many places, such as U-shaped valleys (streams make V-shaped valleys; glaciers scour the hillsides to change the shape of the valley), moraines (piles of rocks pushed by glaciers), and cirque lakes (lakes in the mountain bowl where the glacier started).

FUN FACT: Although glaciologists, scientists who study glaciers, note that ice glaciers have virtually disappeared from the Great Basin, rock glaciers still persist in several ranges. Rock glaciers are basically ice covered with a layer of rock. The rock acts as an insulating blanket, protecting the ice from the sun's heat.

Activity: Glacier Melting

To better understand how rocks insulate a rock glacier, try this experiment. Get two shallow bowls, two ice cubes, and a pile of gravel. Put an ice cube in each bowl. Cover one with gravel. Now put both bowls out in the sun and watch. Time how long it takes for the uncovered ice cube to melt. When it is totally melted, uncover the gravel-covered ice cube. How much of it is left? Is this what you expected?

Places To Visit To See Glacial Features

1. Glacier Trail, Great Basin National Park, Baker, Nevada

2. Lamoille Canyon, Ruby Mountains, Elko, Nevada

3. Steens Mountain, Oregon

4. Little Cottonwood Canyon, Utah

5. Timpanogos Snowfield near American Fork, Utah

6. Palisade Glacier near Big Pine, California

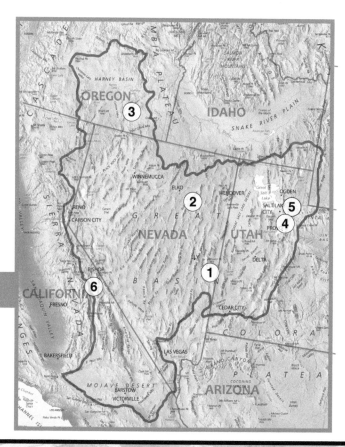

Huge Lakes

During a wetter time about 15,000-35,000 years ago (in the Pleistocene), huge lakes such as Lake Bonneville and Lake Lahontan filled many of the basins of the Great Basin. As the climate fluctuated, the lakes left behind shorelines. Eventually the lakes shrunk, and most of the basins are now dry. Pyramid and Walker lakes are remnants of Lake Lahontan. The Great Salt Lake and Utah Lake are remnants of Lake Bonneville.

Mono Lake in California used to be much larger, as evidenced by the tufa now exposed along its shores.

FUN FACT: Fish and other aquatic species that used to live in these huge Pleistocene Great Basin lakes had to find new places to live as the lakes shrunk. Bonneville cutthroat trout and Lahontan cutthroat trout moved into mountain streams and lakes and can still be found.

Activity: Drying Mud Puddles

Have you ever watched a mud puddle dry and see how it leaves little mud shorelines? If not, here's your opportunity! After a rain storm (or if it doesn't seem like any rain is coming soon, use a bucket of water), check out a mud puddle. Borrow a camera to take a photo of it or make a sketch. The next day, go back and photograph/sketch it again. Do you see any shorelines? Repeat until the puddle is dry. Did the puddle dry at the same speed? If you had some days hotter than others, did it dry faster on those days?

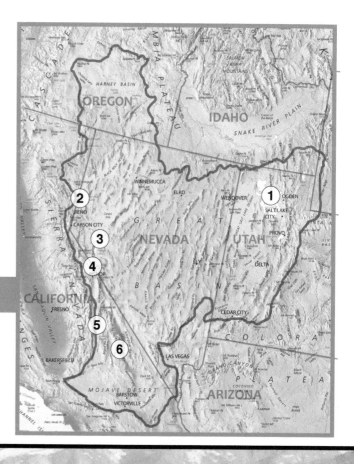

Remnants of Pleistocene Lakes

1. Great Salt Lake, Utah
2. Pyramid Lake, Nevada
3. Walker Lake, Nevada
4. Mono Lake, California
5. Owens Lake, California
6. Lake Manly, Death Valley National Park, California

Sand Dunes

The Great Basin region is also called the Great Basin Desert. When you think of a desert, do you think of sand? Well, the Great Basin Desert does have sand! Much of the sand came from river deltas or huge lakes that dried up over time. The sand was blown into huge piles called dunes in various locations. The size of the sand particles changes on different parts of the dune. Some plants stabilize dunes, while in other areas, dunes may continue moving several feet each year.

Mesquite Flat Sand Dunes in Death Valley National Park, California

FUN FACT: Sand dunes often support endemic species, or plants and animals that are only found on those particular sand dunes. Some endemic species include butterflies, beetles, crickets, and plants such as milkvetch, dunegrass, saltbush, and more.

Activity: Make a Dune

Take a straw to a sandbox. Get low to the sand and blow through the straw. Does the sand go where you want? How long does it take to blow the sand into a dune? For extra fun, take a look at the sand under a magnifying glass or use a magnet to attract the magnetite that may be present in the sand.

Places to Visit to See Sand Dunes

1. Little Sahara near Delta, Utah
2. Sand Mountain near Fallon, Nevada
3. Crescent Dunes near Tonapah, Nevada
4. Amargosa Dunes near Beatty, Nevada
5. Eureka Dunes in Death Valley National Park, California
6. Kelso Dunes near Baker, California

Sagebrush

One of the most abundant plants in the Great Basin Desert is a bush called sagebrush. Over twenty kinds of it are found, growing at a variety of elevations. Many animals make their homes in the sagebrush, such as greater sage-grouse, sage sparrows, pygmy rabbits, burrowing owls, sagebrush voles, Great Basin pocket mice, sagebrush lizards, and pronghorn antelope. Many of these animals have adapted to blend in with their habitat so that it is harder for predators to find them.

The black-throated sparrow finds its home in the sagebrush, along with many other animals.

 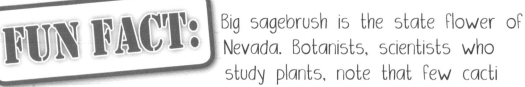 

Big sagebrush is the state flower of Nevada. Botanists, scientists who study plants, note that few cacti live in the Great Basin Desert; shrubs and grasses are much more common.

Activity: Smell a Sagebrush

Find some sagebrush. Squeeze the leaves between your fingers. Smell your fingers. What does sagebrush smell like? Does it smell different if it is wet?

Places to Visit to See Sagebrush

(1) Sheldon National Wildlife Refuge, Nevada

(2) Hart National Wildlife Refuge, Oregon

(+) and most basins and ranges

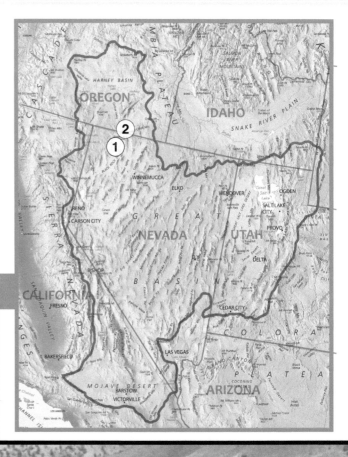

Playas

Playas are dry lakebeds and are sometimes called hardpans. After rain or snow, some playas fill with water. The moisture allows for many insects to survive. This often coincides when birds are migrating, and the birds stop to rest and eat. Look for American avocets, black-necked stilts, phalaropes, and sea gulls near moist playas. After the water disappears from the surface of the playa, it may still be close underneath. Check before driving out onto any playa, or you could get stuck!

Playas are common in the Great Basin. The surface often cracks as it dries, making interesting patterns.

 Land speed records have been set on playas, since they are so flat and smooth. The fastest land vehicle recorded on earth traveled over 760 mph (1220 km/h) on the Black Rock Desert in Nevada.

Activity: Playa Tracks

Stop at the edge of a playa. Can you find any animal tracks? If so, what do you think they are? If not, try this: roll a ball. How long does it take to stop? Now roll the ball on the terrain next to the playa and compare.

Places to Visit to See Playas

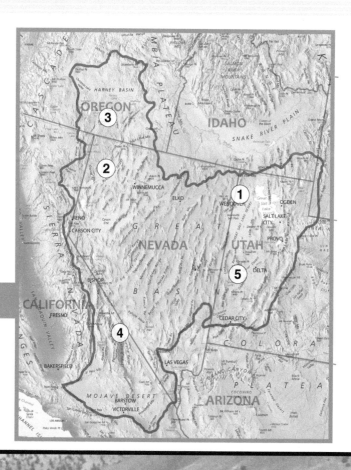

(1) Bonneville Salt Flats, Great Salt Lake Desert, Utah

(2) Black Rock Desert, Nevada

(3) Alvord Desert, Oregon

(4) Racetrack Playa, Death Valley National Park, California

(5) Sevier Dry Lake, near Delta, Utah

(+) And many basins

Mountain Forests

Trees rarely grow in the basins due to a lack of water, but trees survive on many Great Basin mountain ranges. Pinyon pine and Utah juniper are found in the lower mountain forests. You can often see mule deer, pinyon jays, and cliff chipmunks among these trees.

Higher on the mountains pinecone-bearing trees grow in a mixed conifer forest, supporting woodpeckers, mountain chickadees, elk, and mountain lions. Mountain mahogany and quaking aspens are often interspersed. In the autumn when aspen leaves change color, the mountainsides glow with golden and red hues. Periodic natural wildfires help clean the forest.

The North Snake Range, Nevada, in the autumn, looking north to the Deep Creek Range, Utah.

FUN FACT: Ornithologists, scientists who study birds, note that Clark's nutcrackers hide pinecone seeds in the ground so they have something to eat year round. They can remember where each cache is, even though they may have thousands. Once in awhile, though, they forget a hiding spot, and those seeds burst through the soil, starting new trees growing.

Activity: Pinecone Comparison

Find five pinecones from the same kind of tree. Use a ruler and measure how long each one is. What is the average length? Now find five pinecones from a different kind of tree and measure them. Is the average longer or shorter than the first kind? What other differences do you see? If you were a Clark's nutcracker, which pinecones do you think you would like best?

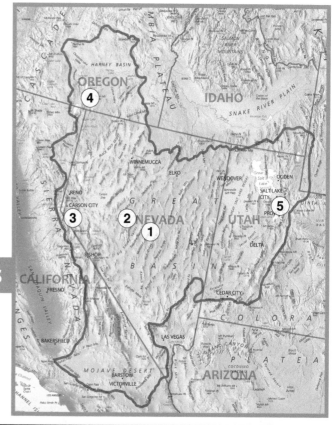

Places to Visit to See Mountain Forests

1. Monitor Range, Nevada
2. Toiyabe Range, Nevada
3. Virginia Range, Nevada
4. Hart Mountain, Oregon
5. Wasatch Mountains, Utah
+. and many more ranges!

The High Country

On the taller mountain ranges, bristlecone pines grow up near the treeline. The oldest ones, over a thousand years old, look nearly dead but still have a strip of green left on them. High elevation lakes may be nearby. The highest peaks don't have any trees, but in the middle of summer have a surprising array of wildflowers. Animals at these higher elevations include gray-crowned rosy finches, golden-mantled ground squirrels, bighorn sheep, and pika.

Bighorn sheep in the alpine zone.

Two hundred years ago, bighorn sheep were common throughout western North America, with estimates of more than two million. Many rock art sites depict bighorn sheep. The population dipped to just a few thousand by 1900. The population has increased since then, but it's still a special treat to see bighorn sheep.

Activity: History of a Bristlecone Pine

The oldest living bristlecone pine, discovered in 2013, is over 5050 years old. What year did it start growing? Use a computer to find out what was happening on earth then.

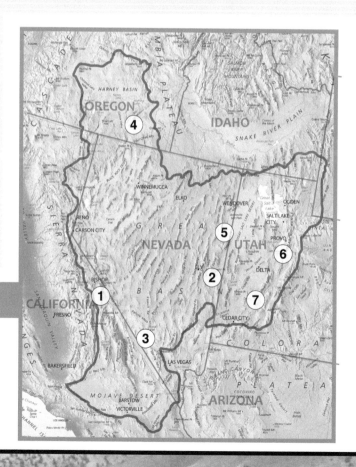

Places to Visit to See High Country

1. White Mountains, Nevada
2. Great Basin National Park, Nevada
3. Spring Mountains, Nevada
4. Steens Mountain, Oregon
5. Deep Creek Mountains, Utah
6. Mt. Nebo, Utah
7. Tushar Mountains, Utah

Wet Places

The Great Basin Desert only gets 5-12 inches of precipitation each year on average, but that is enough snow and rain to feed mountain streams, wetlands, springs, and lakes. These wet areas support a wide variety of plants and animals. Insects such as caddisfly larvae provide food for birds like American dippers and a variety of fish. Also look for tiny snails, beavers, spotted frogs, water shrews, and garter snakes.

Diana's Punch Bowl near Austin, Nevada is one of the many hot springs in the Great Basin.

FUN FACT: Hydrologists, scientists who study water, find that the Great Basin region has the most warm and hot springs of any area in the U.S.

Activity: Learn How an Aquifer Works

Get a big plastic cup and poke three holes in the side: one near the top to demonstrate a spring, one in the middle to represent a shallow well, and one near the bottom to simulate a deep well. Get two containers of water and go outside. Covering the bottom two holes with your fingers, fill the cup with water at the same rate it goes out the top hole. The water you are pouring in represents recharge, or the precipitation that is making its way into the aquifer. While continuing to pour at the same rate, uncover the middle hole. Does water still flow out of the spring? Finally, uncover the bottom hole. What happens? What do you think would happen if there are a lot of deep wells near springs in the desert?

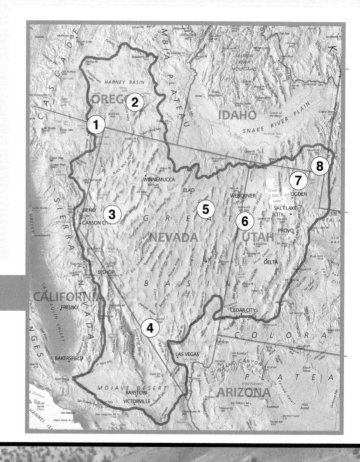

Places to Visit to See Wetlands

1. Clear Lake National Wildlife Refuge, California

2. Malheur National Wildlife Refuge, Oregon

3. Stillwater National Wildlife Refuge, Nevada

4. Ash Meadows National Wildlife Refuge, Nevada

5. Ruby Marshes National Wildlife Refuge, Nevada

6. Fish Springs National Wildlife Refuge, Utah

7. Bear River Migratory Bird Refuge, Utah

8. Bear Lake National Wildlife Refuge, Idaho

Native Americans

Can you imagine living in a place like the Great Basin before cars, television, microwaves, and electricity existed? Many people have lived in this land over time. They include Paleo-Indians, the Fremont, Paiute, Washoe, Shoshone, and Goshute cultures. Archeologists, scientists who study past cultures, can teach us how to find clues about how they lived. Rock art is one clue. Some cultures painted rock to make pictographs. Others chipped away at rock to make petroglyphs.

The Zipper Petroglyph at Parowan Gap, west of Parowan, Utah.

FUN FACT: Pine nuts have been an important food to many Native American cultures. Every fall, many people go and harvest pine nuts in the Great Basin. Excellent crops are only produced every few years, so the collections must be made in different areas from year to year.

Activity: Rock Painting

Find a fist-sized rock and get some paint or chalk. Decide on something to paint or chalk that will leave a message for your great-grandchildren without you explaining it to them. Paint or draw on your rock and see if your family understands your message.

Places to Visit to Learn About Native Americans

1. Eastern California Museum, Independence, California

2. Maturango Museum, Ridgecrest, California

3. Pyramid Lake Museum and Cultural Center, Nevada

4. Grimes Point, near Fallon, Nevada

5. Baker Archeological Site, Nevada

6. Parowan Gap, near Parowan Utah

7. Fremont Indian State Park and Museum, Utah

Explorers and Settlers

The Great Basin region was one of the last places in the world to be explored. John Frémont recognized that the area did not connect with the oceans and called it the Great Basin.

Settlers followed the explorers. Many were Mormons who found homes along the mighty Wasatch Mountains. Other settlers were headed to California on the Oregon, Overland, or Spanish trails and decided to stay in the Great Basin.

Early settlers traveled in a covered wagon like this one outside the Oregon/California Trail Center in Montpelier, Idaho.

FUN FACT:

Historians, people who study history, recorded that in 1848-49, Mormon crickets ate almost all the crops of Mormon settlers. People were worried about having enough food. Fortunately, California gulls came to the rescue, devouring the crickets. The California gull became Utah's state bird.

Activity: Be a Settler

Imagine you're a kid moving to a new place with no houses. How would you build your house? Where would you get to school? How would you get to school? Draw a picture of your life as an early settler.

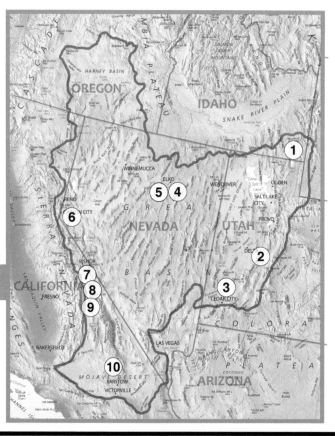

Places to Visit to Learn About Early Explorers and Settlers of the Great Basin

1. National Oregon/California Trail Center, Montepelier, Idaho
2. Territorial Statehouse, Fillmore, Utah
3. Frontier Homestead State Park, Cedar City, Utah
4. Northeastern Nevada Museum, Elko
5. California Trail Interpretive Center, Elko, Nevada
6. Carson Valley Museum and Cultural Center, Gardnerville, Nevada
7. Laws Historic Site, Bishop, California
8. Eastern California Museum, Independence
9. Manzanar National Historic Site, Lone Pine, California
10. Mojave River Valley Museum, Barstow, California

The Pony Express

How long does it take to contact a friend in another city? If you have a phone or computer, you can chat immediately. But before computers, telephones, or even cars, it was more difficult. For nineteen months in 1849-50, the mail was delivered by the Pony Express on horseback. It took ten days to get a message from Saint Joseph, Missouri to Sacramento, California. This was the fastest way available at the time.

You can still follow parts of the Pony Express trail, although some of the route is over rough roads. Every year, volunteers re-ride the Pony Express trail. They carry a GPS in the mochila (backpack) so that you can follow the progress online.

The Pony Express is still celebrated every year with a re-ride held every summer. Volunteers take the mail across the old trail from Sacramento, California to St. Joseph, Missouri.

FUN FACT: Pony Express Riders were usually teenage boys who weighed less than 100 pounds. They learned to cover about 100 miles of the trail at any time of day or night in all weather conditions.

Activity: Today's Mail Route

Write a postcard or letter to a friend or relative in a faraway city. Ask them to tell you when it arrives. Send it by mail and ask the mail person what route it takes and trace that on a map.

Places to Visit to Learn About the Pony Express

1. Fort Churchill State Historic Park, Nevada

2. Simpson Springs Station, Utah

3. Camp Floyd, Stagecoach Inn, Utah

+ Visit stations along the route (route shown in blue on map)

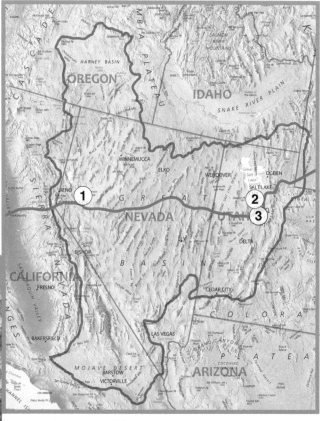

Miners

People crossing the Great Basin noticed strange-colored rocks. Soon miners poured into places, looking for riches. Towns popped up in days and could disappear nearly as quickly. Mining is still an important industry in the Great Basin. Miners dig copper, gold, silver, salt, gypsum, beryllium, and more out of the ground.

Many railroads were built to help transport the ore. You can still find some, like the Nevada Northern Railway in Ely, Nevada; the Laws Railroad Museum in Bishop, California; the Virginia and Truckee Railroad Company in Virginia City, Nevada; and the Nevada State Railroad Museum in Carson City, Nevada.

The Bingham Canyon Mine, located near Salt Lake City, Utah, is one of the largest open-pit copper mines in the world.

FUN FACT: Nevada's nickname is the Silver State and California's nickname is the Golden State. Nevada is now the leading gold-producing state in the U.S. and second-largest silver producer, after Alaska.

Activity: Mine Reclamation

Today miners must reclaim, or clean up, a site when they finish mining. Try this experiment to see how reclamation is done. Put a chocolate chip cookie on a piece of paper and trace its outline. This is the mining site. Use a toothpick to "mine" the chocolate chips out of the cookie. How many do you get? Now, reassemble the cookie inside the outline. This is the reclamation of the mining site. How difficult or easy is it?

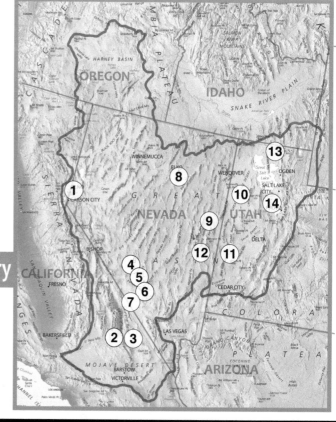

Places to Visit to See Mines and Mining History

1. W.M. Keck Museum, Reno, Nevada
2. Western America Railroad Museum
3. Calico Ghost Town, California
4. Tonopah Historic Mining Park, Nevada
5. Goldfield, Nevada
6. Beatty Museum, Nevada
7. Rhyolite, Nevada
8. Mining tours near Elko, Nevada
9. Ward Charcoal Ovens, Nevada
10. Gold Hill, Utah
11. Frisco, Utah
12. Pioche, Nevada
13. Golden Spike National Historic Site
14. Bingham Canyon (Kennecott) Mine

Cowboys

Many people who live in the Great Basin live near water. Some raise sheep or cattle to make a living. Sheepherders and cowboys go out in all types of weather to move, feed, and care for the livestock.

The cowboy tradition goes to town today with cowboy poetry and rodeos. A huge cowboy poetry gathering is held in Elko, Nevada every January. Rodeos are held throughout the summer in many Great Basin towns.

Cowboys moving cattle in one of the many basins of the Great Basin.

FUN FACT: The term "cowboy" didn't become popular until it was used frequently in fiction writing in the 1870s. Before then, those who worked with cattle were called herders, drovers, or by the Spanish term "vaqueros."

Activity: Cowboy Poetry

Imagine that you're a cowboy rounding up cattle out on the range. What do you see? Smell? Hear? Feel? Think? Write down some words and create your own cowboy poetry.

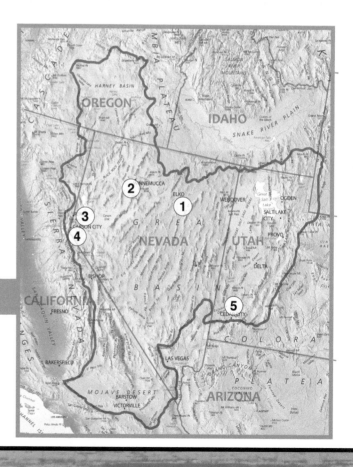

Places to Visit to See Cowboy Life

1. Western Folklife Center, Elko, Nevada

2. Silver State International Rodeo, Winnemucca, Nevada

3. Reno Rodeo, Nevada

4. Dangberg Home Ranch Historic Park, Minden, Nevada

5. Cedar Livestock and Heritage Festival, Cedar City, Utah

+ And local rodeos across the Great Basin

Night Skies

Whatever the reason people live in or visit the Great Basin, no matter the time they were or are here, one thing is the same. The Great Basin encompasses vast spaces without people. That means fewer lights, which means we can see into the dark night skies better than most other places on earth. Astronomers, scientists who study planets, stars, and galaxies, can easily see the Milky Way Galaxy in the Great Basin.

An antenna at the Goldstone Deep Space Communications array near Barstow, California.

FUN FACT: Early cultures made astronomical calendars. It appears that the rock art site at Parowan Gap in Utah may have been lined up to help determine dates for planting and harvesting. Likewise, the buildings at Baker Archeological Site may also have been built carefully to use the changing positions of the sun to tell time.

Activity: Using Stars to Find North

Go outside at night and find the Big Dipper. Follow the two stars in the outer part of the bowl to the North Star. Now you know which way is north, just like the Native Americans and early explorers of the Great Basin.

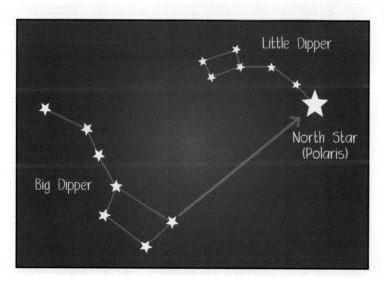

Places to Visit to Learn About Night Skies

1. Clark Planetarium, Salt Lake City, Utah
2. Willard L. Eccles Observatory, University of Utah
3. Stansbury Observatory, Utah
4. Fleishmann Planetarium, Reno, Nevada
5. Western Nevada College's Jack C. Davis Observatory, Carson City, Nevada
6. Owens Valley Radio Observatory, California
7. Goldstone Deep Space Communications, California
8. Desert Discovery Center, Barstow, California
9. Southern Utah University's Ashcroft Observatory, Cedar City, Utah
10. Millard County Cosmic Ray Center
11. Great Basin National Park Astronomy Festival

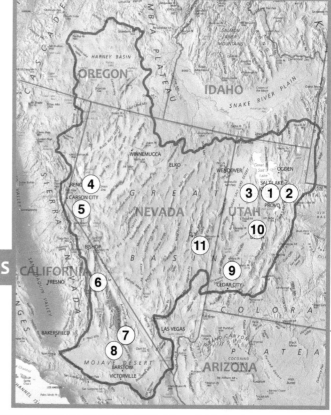

TEST YOURSELF:

In which habitat would the following animals best fit? (Answers at bottom)

A	B	C	D	E

    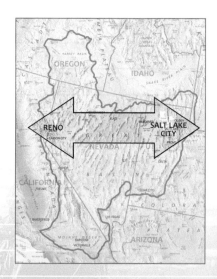

Cave Millipede   Clark's Nutcracker   Horned Lizard   Pine White Butterfly   Fossils

FUN FACT:

The Great Basin area is continuing to get bigger. The distance between Salt Lake City and Reno is growing at about the same rate that your toenails grow.

Test Answers:

A. Millipede: Cave; **B.** Clark's Nutcracker, Mountain Forests and the High Country; **C** Horned Lizard, Sagebrush and near Playas; **D.** Pine White Butterfly, Mountain Forests; **E** Fossils, Wet Places

CPSIA information can be obtained
at www.ICGtesting.com
Printed in the USA
LVHW071949180820
663526LV00002B/22